Whispering

Phillip D. Reisner

Order this book online at www.trafford.com
or email orders@trafford.com

Most Trafford titles are also available at major online book retailers.

Printed in Victoria, BC, Canada.

ISBN: 978-1-4269-1823-0

*Our mission is to efficiently provide the world's finest, most comprehensive book publishing
service, enabling every author to experience success. To find out how to publish your book, your
way, and have it available worldwide, visit us online at www.trafford.com*

Trafford rev. 1/26/10

www.trafford.com

North America & international
toll-free: 1 888 232 4444 (USA & Canada)
phone: 250 383 6864 ♦ fax: *812 355 4082*

I sit quietly alone beside my river
listening to her whisper.

Preface

A better poet I wish to be for within mind and soul dwells thoughts, ideas and emotions wishing to be expressed, but for unknown reasons I struggle to surface and oblige such articulation. I find it difficult to verbalize illusive passions. They lie at tongue tip, mind edge and extraction verge. I wish to warn, soothe and teach through my writing. I seek reason enough to continue my struggle as a poet. I wish others to find a path through my desperate poetic charting. I am compelled to write poetry. I, however, write for myself first and other acceptance second.

My body and mind will softly quell unsettling thoughts when dusk brushes my face and I know that it is time to sleep, but now dawn light seeps through near window wishing to enlighten my restless spirit. Dreams violate my mind at night in bed with covers pulled up around my neck. Imagination streaks through my mind like noonday sun. Writing is like eating an apple. It is sometimes sweet and juicy and sometimes green and bitter. I bite, chew and swallow life. It becomes my poetry from within and based on whispering intent. My purpose unfolds with each articulated living day.

Sometimes I sit quietly alone beside my river listening to her whisper. I feel her ancient wisdom seep into my soul. She flows onward as another million years pass. She makes her way onward cutting deep and wide, then retreats, satisfied with being small again. I began small and shall end small as mind, body and soul finish at initial creation. A tree becomes from a seed. A mountain becomes from a fault. I am a short lived ripple within an ever vibrant river, disappearing quickly into the whole of things.

Contents

Introduction

Perceptions are illusions constructed from thoughts formulated from the smallest particle in the universe called a "wh." "Whs" form creative thought. This process is called whispering. Whispers are the basic matrix that shapes thought reality and articulates creation itself. The whole universe whispers and we learn to listen to help formulate and sustain it. The universe is constantly being thought into existence by this universal pervasive energy. Whispering at its basic level is a spiritual reality thing of which we are all a part. I write about my awkward limited eavesdropping ability in a magnificent whispering universe. I hope we can find some correlation between our individual unique universes. Please now let us listen for wonderful creation sustaining whispers together.

Even God knows my name for
without me He cannot fully exist.

Thought

I can help create, shape, caress and judge.

Form and Function

I took clay and water
from abundant earth and
with hands created a bowl.
I caressed mud with hands,
judged it with eye and
produced form and function.
I was god-like to that bowl, but
created neither mud nor water.
I gave it shape, but
not mind or thought.
I measured its
size and profile, but
not its measured worth.
I controlled its growth, but
not its containing way.
It was an earthen bowl, not a
heavenly fashioned child.

Yet in bowl production
I see similarities to a child.
I can help create, shape,
caress and judge.
I can give God
form and function.
I can help grow
self esteem and value.
I can teach to and
learn from a child.
I can help nurture and
grow a precious child.
I, however, especially must

not misuse, misplace or
destroy a child.
That is a certainty far
beyond a spiritless bowl.

To Be

Separation of willow mean
cuts my depth and
speaks normal segments
like an ancient knife
gently splitting my matter,
yet I feel no pain.
A cutting silver wind song
gently touches temple race and
brings me to life with
malleable artful grace.
In daybreak mist those
silver beads dance
making ancient music when
plucked from a forge and
made into an emerging work.
Large scented bellows make
my heart coals hot enough to
manage steel and soft enough to
create a hunting tool.
I hold my blackness for
only a while, then
yellow, red and white
become without effort.
Willow branches burn,
glory coals heat as a
sward is formed.
A gray shape appears and
slag falls from intention.
I see a main routing base
creating a blue shiny silhouette.
It becomes me and

like sky I again
deep release by
some quenching way that
cools my soul and
ash lays my former grace.

Change Something

I instinctively know that
pure time is melting and
failing beyond control.
Everything is wither changing
like a shifting altering desert.
World events are crashing
down on innocent thought.
And yet I apathetically
sit here with just enough
knowledge to keep me
awake at night.

Weak wrinkled old men
watch clocks spin hands
towards mechanical breakdown.
Innocent children observe
pretty picture calendars get
monthly ripped from a thick
beginning to a one page irrelevance.
And yet I sit here with
clarity within grasp and
just enough wisdom to make
me think too much.

Time has no meaning
between old and new.
I know time is purity
precious within middle
failing unawareness.
I yet sit here with
intellect enough to
peacefully change
something and
too ignorant to
know how to respond.

Stage Right

Circumstance builds reality as
ignorance questions not
how or when.

Time is a dumb one
dimensional thing
seeking only recognition.

Death begins infinitely
far away, before
birth and beyond imagination.

Circumstance a thousand years ago
conjures a future waiting a
thousand years ahead.

How in this enigmatic
whispering imitation does one
seek authentic attention?

Time taps her feet,
ignorance stares and
circumstance plays all characters.

o

Life surely parts
stage curtains as if
knowing waiting future.

Life always seems to
rush onto stage with an
eloquent smile.

Life is a sweet thing with
arms open as if to embrace and
feet dancing as if to celebrate.

She ruefully knows circumstance
begins, proceeds and ends
everything correctly.

Life easily glides about mixing
musical timing with
new born joy lyrics.

Her regal feet move to old wise
recognized choreography with
natural born grace.

o

All anyone can do is
musically move and with
life dance pretend.

Circumstance builds
left, center and
stage right.

Valid self awareness
marks circumstance and
sends life letters home.

Hard maple boards
won't acquiesce or
squeak a tear.

Time wears two hands and
can't legless dance or
serenade circumstance sing.

Judicious lighting conforms,
stage curtains obey and
impostors gracefully bow.

Commitment

With whom will
my crystal mind meld and
in what hand
shall I place
my trust with
commitment waning and
love hiding?
My shadow
keeps washing away as
truthful light shrinks
its wake with morning.
Subtle hints nudge
my thought precious stone
towards doubt in
noon day sun as
sparkle seems to disappear.
I flaunt an anxious gaze and
can't evade enlightenment.
I'm more like a
free bird than a
sturdy tree on
which it sits.
I'm more like a
river than a
dam containing
measured content.
Sometimes I wish to be more
agreeable and compliant.
And yet, most time
I foolishly live where
roses ever bloom and

shadows emit fragrance.
My purified crystal mind
holds me close
like angel arms
on an endless day.

Hope

Hands were clasped,
palm to palm,
in prayer fashion and
knees humbly fell with a
slight throat whence.

Heads stingily bowed and
mouths softly formed,
giving thanks and
asking undue blessings
not for self.

From weak minds
there was little belief, yet
trust matured and
what was needed
got determined.

Then came a voice,
saying, "have faith,
for faith brings hope."
Next meditation for
some time ensued.

Spirit seeped into
minds and souls.
God surely rose,
poured and gushed,
"Oh my," was sighed.

Optimism released insight
like an angel eye showing.
It poured divine passion
about, in and through.
"Oh my," was gasped.

Truth Reveals

Truth takes time,
meanders and twists
through unjust relevance,
creates own existence.
Life is windless waves,
faultless tremors,
unseen warnings and to
where it shall flow
only disillusioned minds
can foolishly tell.
It's like a belief leaning, an
idea coalescing, a
fact confirming.
Truth hides, seeks itself
in obscure visions as a
child sees tomorrow or an
old man hears
his ending gong,
his homeward call.
Church bells ring,
death knells,
truth surpasses and
time waits by design.
Reaching truth and
honesty requires an
enduring strategy.

o

Truth hurts,
makes way in a
downtown theater,
full of drama.
Comedy or tragedy
teaches candor,
causes festering tears
on an elevated stage.
Physical parts and
silent mouths,
sweetly reveal while
obscurity secures
black nights and light days.

o

I walk confusion shore
off a nowhere beach,
scrubbing sandy thoughts,
picking up answer shells.
My mind grinds, but
sand thoughts are building a
beach sculpture slowly and surely.
I learn ocean's wise
purpose and thus my own.
Some can stand here
day and night forever and
not learn a thing, but
I listen, watch and learn
with an open soul that
makes possible future emerge.
My high house
above crashing surf
can't bring me close to

where life begins and
eventually ends.
So I walk a
nowhere beach shore,
seeking, scrubbing and thinking.
Someday that ocean will
feast upon my bones.
I'll be horizon deposited
where sky silently joins water,
where mind reside,
where truth can't hide.

Two Stones

Stones in hand
weigh heavily.
They seek a
resting place, but
cannot be released for
mind holds them,
not hand.

A mind will
hurl them
if decided as
circumstances influence
good or evil fate.

They could be
decoratively placed,
road stone
crushed or even
dividing wall
constructed.
Yet in
standing still time,
they rest in hand,
willing to serve.

Good judgment lies
not in hand,
but in mind.
Good thought
lies not in law, but in
cumulative reasoning.
Stones always endure in
ignorant mode waiting
hand guiding by a
moral or immoral mind.

For Only a Second

Man is a trumpet player
flying high while
escorting doers to a
painting party.

His sweet brass melody
lingers for only an
evolving moment in
time illusion.

His artistic effort
leads others with a
shiny metal gadget
rendering melodic grace.

His persistent struggle for
abiding evolution
fills air with joy like an
evermore rose fragrance.

Somewhere a clock
organizes time while
someone writes music and
angels speak holy, holy.

Man flies towards
ways and means as
sweet constructed sounds
echo through open minds.

Humanity dances beyond
clapping hands and
singing voices while
unison trumpets blare.

Indecision

Piled rocks beside me,
stacked recklessly well,
invite forceful attention as
questions arise and answers hid like
squeamish fallen rose petals
collectively dirt dying.
Those faking anger rocks have
no answers while lifelessly laying,
manipulated and dominated.
Mental rocks and rose blooms
flit through my wary mind.
I sit waiting with anxious notions
like a gardener's hands
seeking earthen planting.
I ponder whether to
hurl vengeful rocks or
gather forgiving rose blossoms.
Middle ground speculates for
it cannot see, hear or speak, and
in this state of mind,
neither can I plant,
cultivate or harvest.
I sit in quandary steep and
must before long taste
decision's bitter results.
Resolution evades mind,
hesitation erodes heart,
vacillation sickens soul.
Deep down inside I know
goodness must prevail.
Rose bushes onward live and

piled rocks are forever dead,
my labored soul reasons.
Mother and father rose twigs
planted long ago,
yet engender wisdom.

Little Spider Bite

A yesterday spider bite, yet
morning itches after a
silent secretive attack.
A small tickle can turn into a
significant mind irritation.

Life's irritations like spider bites
can become frustrations and
then considerable angers.
An undetected spider always
moves to another reticent place.

Spiders leave slight touches.
Their silent venom seeks skin,
blood and mind.
A trivial touch can effect with
migrant poisonous significance.

Only deceptive time can tell how
far a toxin will travel and to
where it shall inevitably reside.
Small implications foster
anonymous consequences.

An irrelevant spot can become a
deadly stain if left to bleed.
One can scratch an itch,
soothe a festering irritation, but
must doctor an apparent wound.

Mindful Beasts

I say no to those
gathered beasts
surrounding my
rowdy campfire.
They seek my
soul this night for
I have not paid
my dues or
sought my
goals well.
I listen to
gathered arguments.
My heady suitcase
beasts will soon
lie dead.
My earthly fire
dwindles as
ancient time
grows reality nearer.
I forever love
piling fuel and
poking red hot toil.
Energy burns in
many ways and
mine is like beasty logs
thrown haphazardly.
I fear soon
I will succumb and
time will quench
my face, my grace,
my soul.

I shall weep
like a baby and
my tears will defeat
mindful beasts lurking and
quench a fire I'll not need.

Now Quiet Hands

A hundred stories
my hands could tell if
only they could speak.
Character scars
silently bear witness
like mind possessing
manuscripts, yet
lacking ability to
willfully express.

My hands learn and
teach an internal faith
conceived from
fear and chance,
insight and ignorance,
faith and hope.

They gracefully part to
embrace moon, sun and
stars, but unwillingly
applaud a dead man's
dignified tomorrow.
A thin space between
yesterday and tomorrow
discloses reality.

My true reality
opens, bends and
flushes that space of
faithless impurities.
I attain true purity

when my hands accept
authentic responsibility
while grasping jagged
mountain side edges.

I now no more gather
character with
withered hands for
today I relent to an
unending restful moment.

Be still now
hands that seek
more than can be
imagined.
Grasp no more for
nothing more is
attainable here.
Speak if
you must for your
spirit is sorely
speechless.

I am gathered ancient
whispered dust on a
partly worn rounded
mountain side.
I help wear
purity into existence
one remembered ash
handful at a time and
with wordless speak
silent dignity is within grasp.

Short Shadows at Noon

Imagination ceased like an iron bell that wouldn't ring or a tear that wouldn't fall.

It acted like a discovered lie at beginning morning or ending night.

It demanded answers to short shadowy questions from thinking men who sought success.

Black dusk silhouettes questioned red clouds that thwarted achievement by shear distraction.

But, morning sang her sweet melody and painted fervent ideas across a radiant sky.

She was a naughty phenomenon unwilling to sleep with anyone yet in love with everyone.

She broke hearts and made grown men cry for in their weak psyche she whispered, "I love you."

She taught everyone to fall in love with sweet imagination instead as if shadows didn't exist and light was endless.

Morning pushed blackness westward, stolen light returned and minds remembered dreams.

Questions threw their haunting elongated shadows, cloaked in black night remnants, towards bright mid day.

Morning answered, noon day sun relinquished and evening
reduced shadows to blotches at thinking men's feet.

Imagination returned like a new bell clanging, a virgin joyfully
weeping as impish morning influenced everything all day.

Three Stones

I carried three polished stones in
my front denim pants pocket,
wore a wide brown leather belt
around my small waist and
carried a shiny brass compass about
my neck nearly every day when nine.

I discovered an old broken rifle in
our unused barn tack room,
planted discovered gourd seeds in
our summer vegetable garden and
found a hundred dollar bill in my father's
secret desk drawer when twelve.

I watched blue cigarette smoke
rush from my rebelling lungs,
looked at soft pornography in a
friend's closed door bedroom and
watched a life changing car wreck happen
before my scared eyes when fifteen.

On and on life organically flowed
like growing a hopeful garden or
writing a novel with no ending and
before long I was many years old.
I yet discover and value as if it is
sweet yesterday on that childhood farm.

Those rocks would be ever shiny now.
That belt wouldn't fit my expanded waist.
That compass would be tarnished, yet
pointing northward giving life direction.
Memories endure, becoming soul parts
like eaten vegetables or written words.

Web Spinning

I have a few years to
spin my web,
assemble my home,
seek dream fulfillment.
With hands and mind
I seek achievement.
With eyes and tools
I construct joy.

Like a spider gliding on
soft woven space,
I mathematically conjure,
physically replicate,
spiritually accomplish some
intended whispered design.
I enter into nature as
it passes through me.

It heads for another place as
I follow buried fertile instincts.
I think, see and handle that
which is guiding me and
construct a gracious web where
I precariously live.
My foolish feet lightly step onto
lighted glistening pathways.

Wispy threads vibrate like
tuned strings causing
structured rhythm.
I spiritually dance,
spinning time and energy with
humble naive intention.
Days pass without notice
until seasons change.

Passing years impinge light,
weaken life's lace,
interrupt everything.
Wisdom leaches inward as
reality seeks itself through that
same intended whispered design.
I yet precariously spin as if a
few years will last forever.

Where Tomorrow Hides

"Stand tall young man,"
someone said.

Tomorrow is past that mental
earthly rooted tree and

behind that inflexible rock,
I reluctantly suggested.

I later discovered that
tomorrow is found in

deep blue clear water, seen
through spiritual goggles and that

it flows as far as a
soul can swim.

> I now like to
> move smoothly in
>
> life's flow with no
> fear of being
>
> ditched or scuffed.
> I like to swim
>
> with least resistance
> one stroke at a time.

"Flow quietly old man,"
someone says.

"You've found where
tomorrow hides?

Composed life

Curiosity

An inner voice asks why.
Time teases revealed answers.
Mind is unrelenting.
Morning sun hides behind trees.
Shadows wait their turn.
I think, question and wait.
Wait for what?
What?
I am not content with what is.
Why?
I am searching.
Answers are concealed.
Where?
Inner voices whisper.
Darkness haunts growth.
It overshadows future.
I don't know answers.
They will come some day.
When?
Ideas coalesce.
Reflections are now real.
How?

Focus

On edge ideas whimper.
They creep mind forward.
They merge into sub-consciousness.

Sun peaks through trees.
Shadows develop.
They lengthen with time.
My mind sees them grow.
I gain intentions.
I focus on one idea.
I am myopic.
I am driven.
Answers seek structure.
Systems gain obedience.
Lateral and vertical merge.
Real and fantasy blend.
Shadows lengthen.
Revelation excites smiles.

Continuity

Practice makes perfect.
Every day seeks tomorrow.
Sun bursts through tree voids.
Ideas flourish.
Over and over I think.
Under and under I realize.
Through and through I reason.
Long shadows shorten.
Sun burns overhead.
Into soul I search.
With spirit I pray.
Ideas gain strength.
Stability connects.
Leaves are too numerous.
I count blessings instead.
I become better and better.

I grow.
I apply knowledge.
I lose own shadow at noon.
I gain it back at dusk.
My days are too short.
My mind is vacillating.

Dialogue

To self I listen.
I can hear leaves rustle.
Mind winds torment.
A storm is always brewing.
I sketch my sky.
I take pictures.
I develop time through space.
I advance civilization.
I am shadows.
I am illusions.
I hear own soul whisper.
I know reality doesn't bleed.
It doesn't swear.
It is shadowy.
My sketches fade.
My pictures disappear.
My sun laughs at me.
I laugh at myself.

Motivation

Compulsion seeks morning.
Rules beg breaking.

Shadows never speak.
I still hear wind.
I feel rain.
I know sun blazes.
I walk onward.
Through forest I study.
Trees are thick.
They leaf too much.
I only see sky spots.
Blue never brings me down.
Clouds are inevitable.
I am always hopeful.
Day pushes me onward.
I will not forfeit my shadow.
I am motivated.
I will succeed.
Dusk waits.
Tomorrow brings another sun.
I usually believe.
Sometimes I suspect.
Intellect tricks.
Reality leaf whispers.
I can feel mind breezes.
They will not rest.
My leaves droop hang.
Fall rules are devious.

Trust

Gut feelings are real.
Have a real one.
It's not an expression.
It's a survival mode.

Self belief buys time.
Ideas grow internally.
Integrity seeks optimism.
Nature respects everything.
Good and bad are friends.
They live together.
They trust each other.
Balance is good.
My gut says so.
I seek diversity.
I create shadows.
I accept illusion.
I trust own reality.
I mistrust understanding.
I trust little outside.
I know much inside.
I am going to heaven.
That is all I really know.
I trust my gut.
My ideas are percolating.
My spirit is calm.

Commitment

I seek truth.
It reveals slowly.
I grow with time.
A forest grows slowly.
I walk a path.
I will not waver.
I challenge self.
I move with ease.
I learn to crawl.

I learn to walk.
Through forest I stroll.
My shadow is long.
My pace slows.
I see tree edge.
Leaves are turning golden.
They fall at my feet.
My ideas are fading.
My motivation is lost.
I singularly commit.
I quietly remain.
I whisper like a breeze.
I don't mind falling.
I drift instead.
In leaves I rest.
I have no shadow.

Unity

I am in isolation.
I drift like a leaf.
I am shadow weightless.
Vision light guides.
I seem to shrivel.
Through blackness I move.
Towards light I drift.
My soul remembers.
I am mind only.
I lose my trees,
I lose my path.
I drift only inward.
My withered voice is gone
My creativity is forfeited.

My earthly ideas vanish.
Spiritual knowledge grows.
Trees are naked.
Green leaves don't exist.
Reality is needless.
Sunlight teaches.
Illusions are real.
My path ends.
I am home.
Life is complete.

Spirit

I never wing walked and felt true chilling air.

Water and Sun

He mashed face into
muddy earth,
softened with tears.
He wrung
heated sore hands,
hardened by friction.
He raised eyes
towards heaven and
provoked insight.
Life's timing is a
mystery.
Wind, water and sun,
torment earth into
submission.
Some days only
God can make.
Some days man
cannot accept.
He wore his
wrinkled black suite
poorly.
Soiled pant knees stained
willingly.
Praying hands clasped
reluctantly.
Sunlight streamed
graciously.
And when all was
said and done,
life went on.
God spoke only

"because," and
he accepted tormenting
wind, water and sun
into his life, but
grudgingly.

Gallows Wait

I see no gallant
radiant purple rush.
Blue sky possesses few
lingering clouds.
Rot cheats weathered
wooden gallows
waiting another neck.
No one lives here.
Many have died here.
New glistening hemp is
perfectly tied and
ready for business.
Calculated weight, distance and
stature is accepted.
No one pleads innocence or
asks for redemption.
Guilty verdict spreads like
wildfire through hearts of
those needing retribution.
Reason hides her empty face with
furrowed brow while
revenge flies high as a
blue rushing hero.
Into minds like a
vanishing sun, sorrow
trickles from hearts.
It silently weeps and
looks for understanding.
It lingers within
cloud cluttered minds and
threatens stormy responses.

Yet like a stone it endures.
Evil gallows wait sorrow in
humble ransacked way.
Innocence yet lives beyond
ugly destruction.

Holy Tourist

An earthly tourist climbed a
long spiraled cold steel
constructed stairway.
Slippery placed steps
hampered effort to see
through an open gazing window.
Night stairway seemed to
ever impede, but finally
surrendered and lifted this
weary would be holy tourist
to heaven's entry room.

He warily stepped through a
faintly lit doorway and
into a yellow painted bedroom.
Angels stood near a bed
waiting to place pure hands
on placid sleeping temples.
Soft silk and down layers of
pastel bedding waited
like gathered flowers
preparing a place where
wisdom's pillow also waited.

An awakening morning sun
streamed through a
far window past
final bed, doorway and tread.
Through that window he gazed,
seeing life anew and
future cleverly clear.
A blooming desert
lay before in
scattering myth and
illusory gathered sovereignty.

I Walk With Angels

I once floundered like a
spawning grunion in foaming surf,
distant dark horizon unaware.

o

I then water edge waded,
in life's beginning,
seldom challenging crashing waves.
I held anxious breath often.
I noticed horizons too well and
feared tomorrow clouds,
yet I rushed toward them as if
some heavenly clock
signaled a brewing storm and
I desired its eye.
I dreaded becoming a mutated
mankind manifestation,
destined to experience an accepted
final calamity too soon.

I then learned to stare into
unforgiving mirrors and
see true reflection.
I saw historical images of
gray hair, lined face and
speckled blue eyes.
My image was a book cover, yet
inside memories resided,
wisdom clashed with my
grunion-like buried essence.

I became a heard song, a
sketchy allegory, a
written adventure novel.
Less time provoked expedient time,
time enough to remember,
sing, listen and write.

o

I now fear a bell tolls in
distant church with
reminding knell.
My own intimate resonance
is a small hand bell
ringing true as if
never losing unique tenor.

Like old rusty fasteners,
thoughts hold me together,
hold my mind together.
I'm an old jetty
reaching outward,
farther than ever before,
into unfamiliar
cold salty deep water.
This extension makes
my spirit roar and
awakens my soul.

o

In these final years,
I wish to actively live
until tomorrow, tomorrow.
I ignore storm clouds and
clocks again.
I watched them too well
between childhood and maturity.
I don't do that anymore.

A wrinkled road map face
reflects journeys taken and
exciting pathways coursed.
Reflection provokes opportunity.
My speckled blue eyes
show every physical injury and
ignores suffered mental pain.
I have no body or mind limp.

I walk with angels at my side,
through green pastures and
lay beside calm waters.
I seek introspection for
knowledge sake alone.
In early morning I arise to
see life spawn and die,
spawn and die.
I am blessed with so many
wonderful aging signs and
remain much alive to flaunt them.

Greater Effort

I sought a greater effort,
down by where
men become and
old men die.
Rivers meet and
land is changed by nature
starting with
one rain drop.
I stood on a levy
waiting for it to break and
it did to my surprise.
I thought it
would never happen.
I was just showing-off
don't you see?
I learned one thing that day,
don't seek a greater effort than
can be lived with or died for.
Yes, down there where
men become and
old men die is a
place to not romance.
There are only dead heroes and
all rivers sooner or later
become one with
something greater.

Melting Ice Cream

Sometimes circumstance
melts like daylight
before darkening eyes as
might a weightless mind
seek obscure explanation.
July ice cream melts easily with
no redeemable excuse.
Life too soon turns milky,
drips onto hot asphalt placed
long ago on a cool March day.
Paved circumstance waits
destined tragedy like
milk, eggs and sugar
wait to become ice cream,
turning, turning into
some pleasure donation.
Life circumstance flows no matter
how frozen it becomes, and
through process on a
September quelling morning,
it can't melt away worry.
Circumstance might
be delayed, but like ice cream
it remains right for
eating just before melting,
even on a January afternoon
full of fix and freeze,
lacking daylight,
meaning and reason.
Sweet cool taste on mind can
fool insight and reality.

Circumstance feeds life
no matter how
solid it seems and
time melts meaning
no matter how
sweet it might taste.

New Self

Broken earthly spirits lie
fallen like drinking glasses
shattered into a hundred pieces,
as if existence didn't matter.
And yet therein lies
holy value of all things,
moral significance in
all broken entities.

Forgive trembling hands,
frail human clutches,
clumsy drops.
In a million pieces
beauty is found
through glass light echoes and
subtle reflecting possibilities.

In collected, melted and
transformed useful glass,
a constructive kiss remains.
Pure and holy ghost renewal
becomes a remade memory.
From melting crucible pours
new chance, beginning and self.

A broken spirit
revitalized and restored into a
smooth decorative essence,
provides an inner continuum
holding serene soul.
Drink on Essence Mother,
your glass is well
half full.

High Hill

Humble are those
strong enough to
stand as gentle
sloping high hills,

braced against
brash winds,
evil hail, beating and
bantering society;

hills resilient enough to
not become sterile
flattened planes on
which to mindlessly

graze cattle and
ugly beasts of
unknown origin, but to
tenaciously survive as

rolling hills, to
persist as beacons of
weathered earth
marking land and sky as

forgiving outer places for
humans to carelessly lie
watching clouds, and as
inner places to

consciously provoke charity,
sanity and self amnesty; and
be hallowed places for finding
natural humanity.

Designer Dress

I cleverly see dawn in
your blue eyes, on
your smiling mouth, about
your quiet attitude.
Always something is
wholly there as if
curious calendars
can't wait and
I'm a master assistant
morning brink working.
Your colorful
curiosity dress flows
while quickly passing time
leaving me gasping.
I can't tell where
dawn ends and day begins.

Oh sweet daybreak
last forever for
I simultaneously touch
earth and sky with
eye and hand ease.

I have become a
curious man, with
all that color and
bewildering circumstance, yet
I remain transfixed,
enchanted so to speak,
by frail reality and
solid infinity.
I simply help you dress.
I'm no designer.

I fix hair, polish shoes,
cook breakfast and then watch
you stream into vanishing day.
My eyes are then empty.
My soul is then full, but
I fear there's no tomorrow

Help Me Do My Best

Strong winds twirl ashes in
scattered display.
They cannot be stilled.
In some dark place found,
they refuse to quietly be.
I can feel them clutter
my head while sleeping.
Ashes laying without me and
I without ashes,
makes my heart ache.
How can I manage time?
How can I manage life?
I'll place them where
God can see and angels
come to bless my
praying wish come true.
Oh take me with and
make me part of
those ashes some day.
For now I say farewell and
scatter them in
passionate wind.
What else can I do?
I would rather with them wash
my face and let them
seep into my soul.

I wish to never again be
without them, but I know,
I must put them to rest,
lay them in comfort array with
deep inviting love.
Someone please
help me do my best when
I feel my worst.

Wall Writing

It's an art unto itself on
cave walls and cliff faces, on
city caverns and train cars.
It traces man's history and
tomorrow's dreams.
It changes minds.
Who are these philosophers with
meaty protesting minds?

They draw, explain and document.
Some educate and expound with
glares, shines and blames.
They make hearts sink, sore and die.
Some leave cold ideas.
Some cause burnt thoughts.
Who are these philosophers
silently printing and drawing?

They are place thinkers
living near gathering edges,
artists making graffiti comments
on waiting blank entities.
They are humanity recorders.
They are truth-seekers
making crashing waves on
dry innocent artifacts.

An Altering Gift

He stretched his ailing mind,
found a new idea in a
back street bar where
some unknown songster
picked a worn guitar.
It was like an epiphany, a
soul awakening experience, a
faith keeping living reason.
His mind became a gateway to
his soul and his soul a
humanity expressing tool.
And in night smoky air, at a
small table with empty beer bottles
left uncollected,
spirituality seeped to forever
change a latent songwriter.
An old unappreciated
black man with no
ambition except to tell stories
stretched and reached for stars,
made earth reason glow in a
way few understood.
A not-ready world
ignored his talent
except one young man with
vision and knowledge.
Revolutionary genre coalesced
where confusion sowed rhythm,
where frustration and despair
cultivated soul.

It was like a personal dawn
arising from darkened ambition.
It was a career beginning that
would span sixty years.

Thoughtful Gleaner

I can glean
empty harvested
wheat fields of
fallen ripe grain and
scuff through
abandoned stalks, but
I cannot within
find lost passion or
forget diminished love.
She brushed and
ground my face.
She scattered my soul in
windy haste and when
wheat became bread, for
some reason or not,
I lost my appetite.
Harvesting love and
baking marriage can make a
grown man cry.
I contemplated
self pity like
scattered wheat grain
left for decay, but
instead reasoned that
I'm surely not
golden abandoned stalk,
fallen lost grain or
stale tasteless bread.

I'm a whispering energy that
makes new stalks wave, a
thoughtful gleaner who
collects waiting seeds, a
lost passion planter who
regenerates love.   .

Ceremonial Shifting Sand

On beach sand two stood with
wind wafted hair and
sun caressed skin.
A purple dressed chi imparted
vowed words repeated that
provoked ceremonial origin.
Waves crashed,
sand shifted and a
living ocean altered.
Meeting eyes stared,
exchanged vows promised and
forever one day at a time became.
Uniqueness was protected,
specialty cherished as
yielding honesty caused
shared humanity to be like an
ever changing sea,
evolving, living, agreeing.
Sand mounted,
altered sea grew and
Kailua Beach waves crashed.
A shore became supple as
ancient sea assurance
narrated again and again.
Two into one became
less into more found.
A sharing life way lured
humility into one aspiration as
security met togetherness and
kisses found a place to be.

Aloha leis were exchanged,
hand upon hand laid and
ring and ring passed while recited
Pablo Neruda love poem coalesced.
Two like wind blessed sand
shared never ending sea rhythm.

Coffee House Blues

I want to slow my day,
quietly remain here and
not go to work.
I contemplate in
my coffee house a
respite from boring life and
distasteful labor.
My eyes surf passing souls
incased in all human
shapes and sizes,
seeking beginning day evolution.
My mind time wonders and
space gathers like an
hour glass seeking its end.
I wish to turn it over,
turn myself over and
liberate time and self.
I see graceful sand shifting,
flowing like exhaled sighs,
wishing to ever flow
essence life pour.
I pretend all needed is a
gentle caress, a soft nudge to
right myself for new intentions.
I travel into what might be called
reality ignorance, for I truly
wish to hammer away at time and
not be gentle or abiding.
I imagine stopping time or
at least slowing it with
magical glass held resolve.

Instead I sip last cold coffee,
say good-by to fantasy for
awhile and coax mind to
accept bitter tasting reality.

Moon Light Ice Dancing

Onward dancing moon light,
push me past piled high snow,
through white conduit mazes and
sincere refracting pathways.
My silhouette races across ice
seeking binding freedom lace.

I see intimate melding of
internal thoughts that create
like frenetic artists
painting frosted images on
mental window panes as if
guided by nature herself.

Feeble intentions race onward
pretending to ease my future and
put my past at rest.
 I pray a full moon to
not break my eyes or scatter
my words beyond tomorrow.

Too soon I'm blind and
cannot feel my gliding feet as
moon light dwindles and
darkness becomes that
bogus artist threatening
my self esteem.

I now fearfully skate in a
veiled valley where disguised
charmers stroke my brow,
speak sweet words and
fill my eyes with false beauty
never experienced before.

o

Skates are broken,
ice no longer remains and
darkness will not disappear.
My shaky mind dwindles like
once piled high snow being
transformed back into water.
Transition is at work now and
I am helpless to mend reality.

o

I won't be snow and ice or a
would be moon light skater
hopelessly disappearing into
some distant gaping hole as
darkness steals refracting light and
frost slows my dancing mind.

I'll wait for a new moon
because skating prolongs
my hyper captive soul.
It satisfies those charmers,
artists and intentions inside
my waiting windowed mind.

I know I can again skate,
appreciate moon light and
glide through life's mazes.
My whispered existence spirit
beseeches fulfillment and
moon light dancing returns.

So onward dancing moon light,
push me past piled high snow,
through white conduit mazes and
sincere refracting pathways.
My silhouette races across ice
seeking binding freedom lace.

Return

Yesterday sunlight does not exist.
It melancholy lingers in lost time of
what could have been and what will be.

A morning breeze flows through an
open window one time then moves
freely onward to another place.

A realized moment escapes
like yesterday warm sun and
today morning breeze.

Life is an evolving moment
faintly remembering itself and
time is ignorant and cannot learn.

Unlike light, wind and illusion, a
spirit can miraculously return and
present itself in future passing days.

And when stones are ground to silt and
feeble men bravely sing no more,
life wisely conceives itself anew.

Some things are never to be again,
others return in soulful grace to
spiritually tend heaven and earth.

My Elusive Mind

I heard howling wind
outside my cabin windows
embracing trees and
pure rain washing my roof.
I slowly fell asleep
thinking about tomorrow and
how another valued day
might be recorded and
engraved in my
introspective mind.

I cannot softly touch or
even aggressively search for
my elusive mind and yet
I value it above
family, friends,
real estate,
gold, silver or even
time itself.
I know without mind
there is nothing, nobody.

My universe does not exist
without mind awareness.
My personal God does not
exist without mind.
I pray to not lose my mind,
carelessly forget it
during night's sleep or
allow another to put it
in some secret place beyond
where I can sanely travel.

Even trees and
rain know
I seek their celebration,
their sweet thrashing and
washing of mind.
An evolving universe,
with mystic grace,
knows my vibrating ways
because I surely recognize
it into existence.

Even God knows
my name for
without me
He cannot fully exist.
Oh how precious
my elusive mind is
with all its
faculty and power,
wonder and grace,
influence and intrigue.

Onward Silver Moon

Gone is my ambush way
Pushed towards grave vanity
Gone from blue yesterday
Where I honed sanity

I saw light of day
Mind sought an advent
Head began a new sway
I became relevant

    Push onward silver moon
    Light my dark way tonight
    Make me yesterday's noon
    Put me on the next flight

I crave successful ways
Now that I'm adjusted
Yet I know life betrays
Sitting here mistrusted

Don't need this awkward way
Cured of childish right
Knowing day dreams betray
And sanity is right

    Push onward silver moon
    Light my dark way tonight
    Make me yesterday's noon
    Put me on the next flight

I was better off gray
Black and white always blends
In woven middle fray
Like a willow tree bends

Send me to yesterday
Where there's infinity
Where my soul ever stays
In nonconformity

    Push onward silver moon
    Light my dark way tonight
    Make me yesterday's noon
    Put me on the next flight.

Muted Murmur

In muted murmur
we are conceived and
earth arrive with
anxious cries as if
knowingly taken
from paradise.
From heaven and
into hell we are born.
Into noise and light,
space and time,
good and evil
we are placed.
Only God knows
future trouble
we will experience and
joy and sorrow
we will feel.
As guided spirits,
we are roughly sited and
with tumultuous minds
we insecurely succeed.
Like earthen rocks,
we are sooner or later
surely minced and
made into fertile debris.

And when body and
mind are finished,
like grain and flour
consumed,
we shall soulfully
whimper our way
back to paradise,
with more knowledge
than when on earth
we warily arrived.

My Golden Suitcase

Sometimes my soul speaks
like a black cloud full of
thunder and lightning.
Sometimes it purrs like a
kitten lying in warm sun.
Yet most times
it serves silently,
collecting experiences,
emotions and knowledge.
It's like a
golden suitcase where
everything I mindfully
accumulate is safely kept.
I cannot explain
where soul begins and
mind leaves off.
They blend like warm
creek water flowing into a
cold river heading
towards New Orleans.
I cannot locate either
within body or brain.
It's two earthly
material things
naively containing
two spiritual things in
silent safekeeping
under cover of ignorance.

They shall join into
one when I pass from
here to there like
thunder and lightning.
I shall travel with
my golden suitcase to
where my then shared
earthly and spiritual parts
will temporarily reside.

Speaking Inner Voices

Inner voices speak.
Few listen well.
Wisdom lingers
beyond thought.
It whispers and
murmurs, seeks mind
rather than ear.
It graciously advises
self preservation.

Wisdom stands on
building ledges,
insisting someone
prevent jumping.
Its sanity and reason
holding hands,
pulling mercy to safety.
Ignorance softly pleads that
falling is redemption.

Minds gather thought,
insight and experience.
Souls gather self
through mind.
A true inner voice
has three faces,
but only one mouth.
Hear when listening for
wisdom speaks uniquely.

Webs

Gracious web with all
your white spun intrigue,

send me on a lighted way,
pass my slender unity through a

soft wind accepted porthole.
You're like experienced delicate hands

holding my dusty channeled dreams,
feeling my soft isolated years.

Now take your weightless pattern,
your mathematical desire,

your artful realm and put
them where I can safely ascend.

I suspect you are of my own spinning,
my own mystical thinking.

We are of same woven filament
clinging to perpendicular braces,

never knowing when a resolution
will kill our near silent existence.

God's hand reaches far with
light and wind, with

motion and direction, with
time and energy.

Oh gracious soulful web spun,
support me one more tolerant day.

Mental Itches

Gently hand in hand
two souls pass through
blackened space with only
guiding pin point stars.
They are as two planets,
two worlds, two universes
making their way towards
from where they came.
Tiny mind tickles need scratching.
Simple irritations need soothing.
They lie awake at night asking
who they are and from
where they came.
It's a time question
more than a place question.
It's a spiritual question
more than a space question.
So onward hand in hand
two souls pass through
so called time and space,
scratching and soothing that
which tickles and irritates.
Onward they travel
towards guiding lights,
towards heavenly beacons with
innocence and courage.
They feel soulful tickles and are
willing to spiritually
scratch them, and that
helps define their humanity.

Dare those guiding beacons be
only within their minds?
Dare they travel on a
false whimsical faith tingle?
Yes, they do journey on a
genuine faith itch that
needs scratching

Spring Will Come

Fear thrusts ugliness
through holes created by
slanted news reports,
arrogant experts and
men seeking death.

Words hurt like reckless sticks
bruising fragile minds.
Future creeps in silent swag
while sunlight gently
caresses spring evolution.

Humanity sees through
thin dirty window glass.
It is freezing outside while
feeling spring-like inside.
Courage seeps within clearly.

Those who provoke anxiety
appose enlightenment.
Spring won't willingly wait.
Cautious minds see through
distorted glass-like fear.

Flowers ignore words
wishing to destroy
modern gardens.
Temperatures coax
unrealized fulfillment.

Some boldly scrub clean
evolving time, have
gleaming outlooks and
"In God We Trust"
faith.

Two Sticks

Down inside where
small coals glow, where
wisdom white seeps,
answers for recognition fight and
tomorrow quietly whispers.

It's like two sticks
rubbed together
creating warmth.
Ears can't hear
blue smoke rising.
Onward answers struggle,
outward they clash in
silent battle with sanity,
reality and common sense.
Two stick questions
need careful rubbing and
constructive fanning.
They eventually become
useful flaming
answers like a roaring red fire
illuminating space and
satisfying themselves.
They arrange time and
befall curious minds.
They speak and intelligence is
born like a morning sun
painting itself into existence.
Tomorrow is only an idea today.
It hides like fire until
provoked into being.

And who provoked fire
other than small me?
Who found two sticks?
Who rubbed them together
with only a mind?

Love

I kissed her face and felt her soul.

Cross Kisses

I touched her face with
four kisses placed
like a cross at night:
forehead, chin, cheek, cheek.
It was her way of
saying good-night and
I gratefully did it with
unconditional love.
I kissed her face and
felt her soul.
She a lady at three made
me a young man at fifty:
forehead, chin, cheek, cheek.
She was a
twin daughter
who gave short-lived life
new meaning.
Her sister required
only one kiss, but
I cherished her
with same grace.
Their love kept me
awake at night:
forehead, chin, cheek, cheek.

Those memories,
after all these years,
yet keep me
awake even though
they're gone,
one in heaven at
three and a half and
one five hundred miles
away at sixteen:
forehead, chin, cheek, cheek.
I count blessing
every morning, but
don't cross kiss at night anymore.

Love Lives and Dies

A weighted heavy on mind
dried flower bloom
reminds that love dies.
Like sand grains
between fingers or
night created hair knots,
love surely irritates.

Old love is seldom
physically present yet
mentally haunts like a
pale cold night dream.

It's bottled sour milk
pushed back and
concealed in a
cold steel refrigerator.

It's forgotten
rotten apples
down low drawer sitting and
silently waiting removal.

Oh how well love can be
mind disregarded and
fruit and liquid
willingly rationed.

And yet again another
desert bloom is picked,
warm milk is drunk and
sweet apples are eaten.
A lightly weighted mind
removing mental poison
reminds that love lives.

First Dawn Teasing

I remember first meeting,
watching dawn tease,
waiting love's first light,
knowing first touch.
And, sun quickly rose,
burning day,
baking our loving embrace.
We made discovery love and
found physical attachment
fulfilling.
Afternoon brought
mild soothing grace with
sun allowing
our love to grow and
anxious breathing settled into
comfort and security.
We finally became one,
beginning and ending together,
becoming what we always feared,
dependent upon another.
Now as night falls and
life's melody floats and
rings our future,
we remain yet
able to see first dawn,
teasing our spirits young.

Sweet Rock Hands

Kiss my sweet rock hands
held in silent reserve
until pollen flies from
desperate flowers and
bees make honey in
some hidden place.
Emotions dwell in rejoice,
sweet beyond imagination.
They wait with nothing to
sustain unless by a queen's
instinctive command.

Kiss my sweet rock hands that
pull from an inner world
artfully constructed containers.
These spirited gateways and
honey filled compartments are
emotional mind blessings.
From birth a mother caresses
love created by ever emotions.
Instinctive commanded faith is
like a queen bee seeking
mortality worker effort.

Kiss my sweet rock hands that
separates hardness from softness.
Giving adoring attention is an
ardent emotional gesture that
sweetens an alluring mouth.

Purifying natural ways is as if
honey contained appendages
are from a higher being.
Expressing emotions for a
rock hard man is a
true meaningful life taste.

Dove's Call

Muted church bells ring,
across muddy river's way,
like songs on gusty wind,
they love lost remind.

Whispered words glide on a
sharp chilly breeze felt.
It's a mournful dove call, a
distant train whistle.

It jolts melancholy as
I feel her passion again
beneath steeple soaring,
church bells clanging.

o

Sensibility vibrates
wishful lamenting.
I only suspect her calling
from river's other side.

She's not gently asking and
seeking my arms again.
I fool myself for
dove calls don't exist.

Only painfully clanging
church bells echoing
across muddy river's way
approach my river bank

Importance

Dawn breaks time's silent press,
like a sounding bell awakening,
before again I rush
another day forward.
Does she know her
importance lying motionless?
I wake her with
one soft touch.
Coffee we silently drink on
bed's rumpled edge,
speaking not words,
but giving glances of love.
Dawn makes way
through a near window,
brushing warm light
upon her face
like golden spiritual haze
matching her muddled hair.
I take moments seeking
morning's offered grace and
self forgiveness for
ignoring such importance
earlier in life.
She is like a symphony
softly inner teaching,
light out of darkness,
knowledge out of ignorance.
She feeds
my hungry earthly soul
spiritual momentum food
another hopeful dawning day.

My Mother's Breath

I

In a small bed
I laid nestled beneath a
slanted flowered wall.
Furniture and toy treasures
shadow decorated
my second floor room.
A soft glowing
top of stair night light
cast an attempted
dim calm mood.
A quilted comforter,
under which I lay sobbing,
warmed my misfortune.
To bed without supper
I was told to go and
without a good night
kiss or hug.
I was four years old and
punishment came
like a hammer,
plunging mind into
unknown shadows that
decorated time with
foolish decor.

II

My bad behavior
put me into a
found broken place that
brought truth glaring,
stomach growling,
eyes seeking,
heart searching.
That dim stairway light,
seen through tears and
self inflicted pain,
fell short to soothe
my puzzled mind.
It only helped to conjure
childhood martyrdom and a
false question,
"How shall I make her pay?"

III

Sorrow streaked
like a missile that
suspended reason.
I was a prisoner in
my own room,
enslaved,
too young to escape,
too old to accept truth.
My imagination galloped
unlike my toy horses that
stood motionless on a near dresser.

My mother couldn't
punish with a
iron farm hand that
always touched softly and
held me gently close.
But tonight her
correction spoke a
new language.
My dim lit room
pushed a mother's love a
million miles away.

IV

"Can't she hear me cough?
I can't breathe."
Conjured serious problems arose
beneath colorful quilted warmth.
Trouble loomed without reason.
Hurting, suffering shadows
rebuked silent air connecting us.
"Can't she hear me cry?
I might die."
My pretentious ailment
finally got attention.
She came up stairs and
sat on bed's edge.
She lingered softly,
never asking what I needed or
spoke of why I was there.
She held me for awhile,
tucked my quilt up around neck,
kissed forehead and
said everything would be alright.

V

She remained there a
long time,
mending my heart,
loving me without lecture.
She finally stood and said,
"see you in the morning."
She brushed my hair back with a
gentle touch,
hugged me one more time,
"sleep tight my sweet boy."
With another hug and a
imprinted forehead kiss,
I knew she loved me and to
bed I took a lesson.
She comforted well,
but nothing comforted
better than her warm breath
on my cheek

Time's Reward

Brush my hair from
weathered brow,
furrowed from too much life,
from too much thought.
Take your feathery hand
lightly across my cheek,
make it blush,
make it tell how I feel,
make it resemble my life.
And upon my lips
place your mouth,
speak it not into reaction or
gaze at it long,
just kiss lightly and
with passion felt.
Let night come quickly to
hide my bashful nakedness,
let it bathe my uniqueness,
let it affirm my
life consumption.
Fill my soul with
your own bashful love,
let it seek that place where
we both hide and
where weathered time
rewards.

Permanent Marker

You're like a lost
permanent marker
found when I
had nothing with
which to write.

My future waited
tablet, mind and soul.

I now cherish
writing time and a
future together as
ink and paper celebrate
my poetically guided hand.

Somewhere Roads

She held my hand in
overflowing traffic,
guided me through
risky mazes, and
like a dream,
she disappeared too soon,
letting cobblestones crush
my shy remains.

To somewhere roads are
dangerous without a
helping hand,
without someone
who loves well.
To nowhere roads are
endless soul eating
conduits to hell.

Oh how I wish
her here again with
soft white hands
seemingly so frail.
Her will was
strong enough to
make me brave and
gentle enough to share.

I wish I hadn't
treated her
like a dream, but a
wonderful reality.
She wished only
reflecting love.
I wish her here again to
wander roads forever together.

Raft to Somewhere

I sorely dreamed that
I was down by river's edge.
I found love sleeping
beyond reach on a
wooden raft floating
towards a waiting gulf.
She awoke just in time to
see me beckoning, but
she could not control
raft, water or time.
We gazed in wonton
lover need finding,
half expecting some
external help, but
time, water and raft
drifted onward.
I ran along river's bank
until a wide creek
separated us farther.
I waded across it with
frantic strides, reaching
other creek side, then
ran river bank farther with
fear of losing my love.
She gazed up river as
I dodged trees and
downed limbs in my path.
She was nearly
out of site when

I saw her dive into
muddy flowing water.
I kept running until
I reached where she dove.
I also dove into
muddy flowing water.
I could not find her.
I looked at river's edge.

She stood then on
river bank as
I further floated
fearfully downstream,
out of control,
physically and mentally
drowning from my own
impetuous thinking because
I could not swim.
I managed to pull myself
onto her swirling raft, then
looked back to
see her disappear and
remain out of sight.
I was then in
river's middle as
current guided me
quickly downstream.
Jump and drown
was not a choice.
Maneuver to a far bank
was impossible.

Waiting for my
imaginary lover's hand to
pull me to safety
would never happen.
I floated onward,
loveless and alone on a
raft heading horribly south.

Silhouettes and Hills

I anxiously pace.
You lay on a far hill.
I remember your silhouette
against a moon lit sky.
I have blood on my shoes.
It blends with dirt.

I wave good-bye.
That hill is foreboding.
I imagine peeking dawn.
You disappear within
day light.
I remove my shoes.

I walk silently
away from where
you once stood.
My feet are bloody.
They will not
wash clean.
My soul is lost.

I cannot pray.
My mouth is dry.
I cannot speak.
You are a memory, an
unfulfilled dream.
My soul is bloody.

Life begins and ends
like silhouettes and hills.
You lay beneath mounded earth.
Darkness took your silhouette.
My hands are bloody.
They will not wash clean.

Boomer's Upward Dream

I'm turning sixty, but
feel thirty.
I mentally seek tomorrow
as if it yesterday and
I'm a mischievous boy.
In a daydream state,
I hear rock-in-roll music,
imagine what-ifs and
drive a noisy
purple pimped-out
low rider pickup truck.
My delusional mind is
either far gone or near
uncovered childish insight.

I ask to boldly step into a
waking sky where thoughts
momentarily change and
minds moon-like gravity sway.
Let me influence earth's crust and
let life effect my swelling soul.
Windy way brush my mind,
send me towards tomorrow in a
full white sailed ship with a
blue water bathed rudder.
Let me fall asleep this two AM.
Pull me forward and
lift me towards some unknown
state of mind and place.

There are no secrets now,
no ways to learn,
no apologies to speak.
I gaze far across a
bowed horizon and set my
mahogany boat's compass.
Up and away I rush through
white caps and blue swells.
There's no turning back.
Onward and upward I sail.
Wet distorted eyes
approach black clouds.
I fearlessly navigate into a
broadening dark sky.

A light point then guides me
onward and upward.
Black sea images
desperately fade below.
I sail skyward in blackness,
towards hell it seems,
I, however, cannot resist a
beckoning light.
It whispers my name.
Yesterday can't return.
Meaningless time falls
below and behind
into gloom as a
purple membrane engulfs.

I lower my white sails and
wrap them about my essence.
I am worn rudder released.
My journey is complete.

I sit in boyish humility on
my dead father's spiritual lap.
He strokes my head and
pats my back with
his giant hand.
Tomorrow never looked better.
I guess that my boyishness
will last forever for in
his massive hands I rest as
windy ways cease to exist.

"Dream on thoughtful man,"
someone whispers.
"You'll awaken before long and
see accumulated wrinkles and
feel a fading mind.
Out of control time will
constantly rush into tomorrow, but
you'll participate with a
boyish grin that seeps outward
from a childish mind.
Seek not its demise for through
heaven's gate you'll pass, and
in that purple painted truck with
fat tires and loud pipes you'll ride."

I awaken at dawn with
dream remnants and
renewed vigor haunting.
My mind seeks no agenda or
happiness scheme.
I then launch my
twelve foot fishing boat and
power up stream.

A warm breeze brushes my skin and
sunshine warms my soul.
I feel as if someone special
vigilantly watches over me,
carefully listens to me,
willingly protects me.

Brass Door Knocker

Silent heavy
brass plated knockers
on front doors
beg to be hammered.
Anxious old ones wait alone
behind those doors.

Their frail minds and bodies
can't see beyond
dirty smudged windows
through which they gaze at a
world sliver passing
before dim eyes.

Surely someone seeks
wisdom imprisoned
behind front doors,
where minds wait
visitation and souls know
hope is fading.

Too many find
themselves behind
silent knocker doors with
minds possessing no
dreams, schemes or
configured plans.

Too soon short lived earth
spirits wing their way
towards heaven and
wisdom is wasted by
reluctance to hammer a
heavy brass knocker.

Painted Cloth Coat

Life's lessons came like
alpha to omega
swinging on a tree branch in
my childhood back yard.
A weaver came to
fabricate cloth and a
painter came to
decorate it with
past and present images.
A seamstress came to
create a special coat.
I then wore that
painted shroud as if it were a
living entity.
It became a mental thing, a
description of my spirit and a
protective wrap for my soul.
Vivid colors in bright sunlight
made my spirit glow, but
when I entered that
dimly lit nursing home,
it fought to stay alive.
I was then reminded of
"good old days, "of
days when everyone could
run, jump and dance, of
days when my aunt spoke
loudly a mile a minute.
My reminding time shroud
allowed color sharing,
warmth giving and
dignity protecting.

My spirit sang well being
provoked by life's
internal music.
I then placed my coat on
another's shoulders with
quiet hands and an
empathic sense that
I had just spent time with
my dear sweet mother
who passed a
long time ago.
My sharing swung from
alpha to omega.
Muted lyrics flowed superbly
in tune with a
faint melody and yet
feeble ears heard,
clear aged eyes saw and a
ninety-two year old spirit felt.
I received more than
I unknowingly gave.
I said good-by and
left some color behind.
Everything swung from
ebb to flow,
beginning to end,
alpha to omega.
Fabricated colors of a
reminding whispering shroud
kept me oscillating as if
magically again being a
child swinging on a
tree branch in
my back yard.

When Drumming Ceased

Grace befell humility when
drumming ceased and
welded music broke.
Gold plated brass moaned for
in good time a
trumpet player was
superbly shaped.
From his lips that
silver coated brass
mouth piece got removed.
No more sound
allured anyone down by
river's edge or in
old French styled buildings
standing silently weeping.
To knees dropped humanity and
stone streets weighed
heavy in awkward retreat.
A band stood still.
Another day passed
without recognition.
Welds broke, valves stuck,
artistic reverberation sought a
last mellow note while
drummers lost their sticks.
Dry lips pursed,
empty hands clasped,
wet eyes downward gazed.
Grace befell humility when
trumpeting ceased.

A little trumpet spit and
some scattered sheet music was
only left, but that was
enough for in minds echoed
graceful appreciated notes
sweet as an ear could hear.

Nature

On and on she flows, gashing and grooving.

Ever Changing Nature

She's not just an
intending face, a
quantity shaping grace or a
sliver of earth waiting
precariously to fall.
She's a wave counter, a
stone stacker, a
wind catcher.

o

She whispers,
"waves become seas and
rocks become shores.
Time seeps into time
with no effort or trial."

o

On and on she flows,
gashing and grooving
until music and
rhythm is an
earth commodity.
She's here and
present in all things
new, old and remade.

She evolves and perfects.
Blue covers her soul
while white purifies her mind and
green makes her spirit
different each day.
On and on she flows,
gashing and grooving with
time on her side.

Blind Man's Cane

Mother feels her way through as if
using a borrowed blind man's cane.
Her quiet hands seek revenge.
Her waiting time is nearly gone.
And like flowers that can't see,
she feels her way towards spring,
instinctively tapping and clicking earth.
Tap, tap goes her white lightening with
red striped thunder cane,
swatting dead grass,
displacing fermented leaves and
puncturing damp soil.

Soon she throws her cane away.
With anxious vigor she invites
brilliant soothing sunlight and
calls sweet warm breezes to bear.
Oh how she rejoices with
everyone looking and
letting held breath release.

She then becomes sunlight and
breezes that will not rest.
She becomes that blind man's cane.
She is white paint and red stripes.
She is green grass and trees.
She is lavender soul and grace.
Oh how well she wears her
resurrected beauty while
her hands work soil and rain.

She greets spring with
velvet soft wide open arms while
loving every honest moment.
Her white gown flows across blues skies
while her finger tips touch here and there.

She floats on her own breezes and
makes her swirling way northward.

A humming melody fills waiting air that
touches dancing flower ears,
emerging wheat legs and
budding tree limbs.
Everything seems to sway with
her graceful effort while
listening to her tapping rhythm
one moment at a time.

Shadows

When shadows walk and
see themselves important,
they're like reality
soaking dry deserts,
begging flowers.
When fame seekers bask in
uncensored remarks behind
false flowered screens,
they see self importance and
make angels sing
discontented songs.
Deserts are incomplete and
unimportant without
sand grains,
unable to germinate even
one basking seed.
So when shadows walk,
know they are not
so worthy,
seeking no influence and
knowing no sweat.
Who is much different
than an empty shadow
giving no relief on
censored way?
Perhaps real value is
shadow-less, too
small to noticed, but too
important to forget.

Perhaps sand particles do collectively grow form, function and flower, and create shadows that aren't easily perceptible.

Yellow Bird

Yellow bird on
gathered warm air,
you seek places to be
ever free.
You thwart a tyrant's
desire and
obstruct desperate anarchists
wishing to steal your wings.
You stretch from
grounded trees to
liberated floating clouds as
shadows plunge long in
setting crimson sunlight.
You are a symbol of
freedom flow and
know many
seek liberty's demise.
Frustrated red sky
will only be for awhile.
So sleep well yellow bird
for tomorrow again brings
jealous eyes seeing your
deliberate flight.
Wishful freedom ears
hear your song
on wing tip air rushing.
You give hope for
pliant harmony as
you whisper a
soft morning
perceptive call.

Wild Rose Bush

Let rose odor carry mind,
like wind carries leaves into
drifted piles along a fence row.
Let familiar odors provoke time
revisited along a barbed fence and
capturing woven steel.

o

A wild rose bush grew
farther and farther,
traveling from rooted beginning.
A green trail silently cultivated
itself with innate memory,
fostering thorns, leaves and
small pink roses
within a structured domain.

Fall's revenge lay as rotting
never to live again leaves,
yet rose bush renewed itself,
year after year,
among woven steel
stapled to wooden posts.
On and on it grew,
flavoring air and eye with
sense of humility and beauty.

For fifty years it grew,
like farm children who gazed,
but did not touch its thorny vine.
Longer and benevolently,
it stretched to a far corner post.

Finally everyone was gone,
moved away, grown up.
No one was there to appreciate it.
House fell apart,
termites ate away its
wooden beams and studs,
stairway and doors until once
inhibited structure diminished,
only memories in dirt lingered.
Remains were hauled away,
burned or buried.
Used no more barns
crumpled beneath own weight,
where children climbed and
once played in mounded hay.

Rock driveway disappeared
among weeds and grass,
showing no foot or tire imprint.
Fence remnants humbly hid,
lying in cold wet ground,
half rotted wooden post and
rusted farm fencing got buried.
Wild rose evidence vanished,
its whole splendor gone.
Its gallant vines,
dangerous thorns and
pungent raised flowers gone.

And yet wonderful life odor
remains in aging minds.
Somewhere in distant places
living memories yet reside.
Enduring graceful growth
displayed on hardened fence is
sustained by child like reminisce
living past rose's feral reality.

My River Place

I sit near river's edge
waiting inspiration to
tie body and mind with
salient contemplation.
I wish to weave a
spiritual lattice to
capture my soul's grace.
Muted water murmur
helps speak my netting into being.
Catfish scour bottom
like silent nomadic
prehistoric hungry entities.
I find myself flirting with own
wandering mind frame
seeking, fishing, catching
river's mystical offerings.
I find a vigilant inner place.
My gut clinches,
mind aches and soul burns.
Body becomes a prehistoric
hungry entity while intellect
 becomes a woven spiritual
lattice of contemporary inspiration.
I mentally dive into
muddy water and clearly
see more than cloudy
catfish images.
I see my own dragons and
primordial beginning.
I feel murky current pulling me.

I struggle to remain alive and
preserve mortal connection.
I no longer sit beside, but
bravely swim within
life's murky water.
Deliberation is mine.
My spiritual lattice is real.

Dragon Stones

I wished cool water drawn
by a rope hanging bucket from a
shaded deep dug well.
Body sought quenching while
mind sought comfort.
Placed encircling stones lay like
dragons holding dirt at bay from
seeping collected water.

Into black depth I listened to
hear ripples whisper my name.
I heard not a sound.
Suspicion entered thought.
I pulled hemp rope with
soft calculating hands,
imagining modern times changing
water into wine for my pleasure.

Curved oak bucket pieces with
metal bindings covertly
withered at well's bottom.
That bucket held fate,
teased senses and
secretly warned that
regret can be a
cruel life way.

I pulled hand over hand,
desperately towing while
praying some childhood
broken biblical verse.
That dry rope and bucket
culminated with no shame.
I retrieved no water,
wine or pleasure.

That beautiful willow consumed
all and left nothing for me.
"Who planted that stupid tree in
such a near thoughtless place?"
I angrily yelled.
Expectation often dwells where
dragons live in cheating shade,
high and dry in hell's depth.

It was a selfish oasis and
I an ignorant man searching
among cruel dragon stones and
pliant willow trees for
easy living and
instant gratification.
Body sought quenching while
mind sought comfort.

Certain Winding Path

I walked a certain
conventional path on
tightly woven
hope,
not on solid earth,
but on something
akin to delicate yarn
being wound
over and over itself,
bravely winding into
strength and hardness,
toughness and
completeness.
I stood outside,
not part of,
only about while
delicately balancing on a
beautiful soft fuzzy
dangling filament.
I outer survived an
accumulating world as
neither king nor
peasant or anything
between to self define.
I finally found myself
insecurely balancing on a
plain awkwardly melting
piece of string.
It wind meander with
elements ripping and tearing.

I found life dissolving
beneath my feet as if
artfully designed for destruction.
I truthfully did not walk a
certain path, but a
winding path of uncertainty.

Learning

We spend life
learning after gasping
first inhalation and
before fighting last
wheezing breath.
Life's continuum is an
everlasting erudition
like flowers finding sun.
It is frenetic and intense,
painful and frightening,
relaxed and peaceful.
Life is a constant
letting go and grasping
as might a hand feed a mind.
It is relentlessly changing and
adapting tentative adventure.
Magical bell curves
within mind scrutiny
evaluates and applies skills.
Into a startling world
of ever changing forces
we arrive
naked and screaming,
later leaving
naked and whispering.
We are not unlike
scalded tomatoes
dunked into cold water,
ready for peeling.

We're born with
clothing skin and a
supple working brain and
later buried with
lifeless debris and a
fervently amassed mind.

Day

I fasten day to a
wide black belt,
carrying it around
like I own it,
speaking to strangers,
showing them
how lucky I am.

How many have
such a wonderful gift?
How many know
how to grasp day and
make it their own?
Many are envious,
wishing ill for me.

I laugh at morning and
kiss tired evening
good-night.
I put it aside for a
few hours to rest and
then start all over
again at dawn.

I pray I shall never
forget how to utilize day,
how to capture it and
how to hold on to it.
I pray I shall never
forget its importance and
exploit it to a fault.

Nature Custodian

Beyond brushed dawn,
into seeking dusk,
guardian dirt grinds
abundant earth soul.
I politely sense
with waiting expression
its subtle instability and
deep black security,

I feel valued dirt,
smell it and
know that it
holds tranquil secrets
beyond imagination.
Earth accepts diverse
desert wind whispers and
warm mountain murmurs.

With graceful charity and
benevolent time,
green grass pastures
fill my wetted eyes.
Mountains that groan
softly below surface
hold, nurture and fulfill
inevitable plans.

Oh wary black dirt,
here held between and
within humble hands,
trust my resolve and
allow me to be a
dream grower, a
child feeder, a
worthy earth custodian.

Not So Different

Wind howls in
blackest night
like a thousand ravens
flying through winter
leaf naked
maple tree branches.
Sleep is impossible for
I fear those eighty year old
natural statues might crash
onto my little green house.
They are sweet humanity
lovers during summer, but
naked gray sapless
monster through winter.
They reluctantly sway
without truly bending,
fiercely stand without
seeking knowledge and
instinctively cling
without acquiring fear.
I realize together we
face midnight darkness,
vulnerable nakedness and
accepted uncertainty.
We are not so different except
I can humanly think,
imagine and fear.
I can hear those ravens
screeching vulgar threats in
trees and mind.

I am aware of
naked vulnerability in
time and space.
I also instinctively
remember to be a
grateful human being
bowing to nature.

Time

They grasp like edifices
wishing hopeful endurance.

Black Time

Seeking silent refuge
with black inspiration is
like pushing against
belligerent time at
midnight hour.
Invisible narrow lines
wrap around spinning earth
while invented hours are
held hostages in a
closed wooden box of
shrewd gentle workings.

It's an instrument playing a
squawking melody.
It's a monotonous theory that
cannot prove today is
heading towards tomorrow.
It's a lone communicator
announcing intentional time with
slow moving arms and
attached slender hands
predicting moment by
moment persecution.

Falling night blackens
everything that stands
on floors and hangs on walls.
Shadows grow longer until they
evaporate everything into a
correct nonexistence.
Time moves onward
through pitch black space,
remembering and forgetting.
Each lonely tick
counts life and death.

Accompanying Melodies

Mother's remembered
heart beat yet bonds
like a face brushing
wind tantalizes or a
long ago song
melancholy saddens.
I remember and in
heart can nearly feel.

My little boy psyche
remembers her voice
like a train whistle
calling through thick
night air
near our farm house.
I remember and in
mind can nearly hear.

I used to sing
accompanying songs with
brushing wind,
screeching train whistle and
beating heart rhythm to
own life tempo.
My history frowns and
reluctantly fades.

I feel abandoned
here alone with
only train whistles and
thick night air.
I fear my mind is falling,
crushing and obscuring
memories that
yet make me smile.

Wing Walking

I never wing walked and
felt true chilling air.

I sit watching
too much news.
Too many people
hate well and love poorly.
Depression seems near.
I ride my motorcycle for awhile,
feel better and then
come back to watch
some evening news.
So much yelling to make a point.
So many crying to tell a story.
It seems kind of pointless to me.

I never wing walked and
felt true chilling air.

And then war reports appear and
confusion about how it's going.
They send my favorite
correspondent too close and
he dies without a sound.
Where will it all end for me?
Will I make news and
become news myself?

No, I'll probably fade away in
some little obituary
like my TV when turned off.
Therein lies a matter crux.
Life is mysteriously boring.

I never wing walked and
felt true chilling air.

First and Last

First and last time touches and
sights are never forgotten.
Beyond them lies imagination and
unexpressed passion.
Beyond imagination and passion,
cloaked in black space,
virgin time waits to be explored.
So many wish to see and touch
it's smooth and course affection,
its texture and weight that
causes hearts to sing.
Future quietly well sits
somewhere out there
beyond natural reach.
Minds spin time forward to
touch tomorrow.
And when sweet tomorrow
comes with its rain and sun,
most only gaze farther with
mind for a next tomorrow.
First thrills and fears
impress with short lived
momentary impression and
fleeting expression.
And yet some lucky ones touch
first and last time
over and over again.

They find their own
tomorrow rain and sun that
washes and dries a collective soul.
Their love is a smooth and course
weightless spiritual material of
which life's passion is conceived.

Old Man Fox's Clock

An old cheap yellowed
cardboard faced clock,

discolored, wrinkled and
curled by mean time

crept onward with
worn inner parts ticking

years into decades,
not knowing its cheapness or

poor construction.
Old man Fox

bought it when young;
his then shiny skin reflected

morning sun,
illumined eyes saw

tomorrow's gifts in
endless reckon.

Future's controller
counted daybreaks and

measured seeds planted with
unforgiving patience,

measured consistency and
fairness.

It ghostly warned that
time is always new and

dawn tomorrow is
someone's dusk.

Morning spring loaded
potential into kinetic as

evening yet
onward ticked

towards its end,
towards brokenness,

towards uselessness.
Old man Fox's body

discolored, wrinkled and
evolved towards emptiness,

towards silent ticking,
towards another prayed

naive spiritual beginning,
towards ever time itself.

Dreaming

I live in a secret mind place
where future encounters hide, unlike
granite statue shadows in a
courtyard at night
moonlight moving slowly,
I effortlessly speed dream while

seeking nimble allure.

My mind hurdles voids,
escapes thought residue and
passes to a dream place where
peacemakers elevate tranquility, where
spirits graze selfless meadows,
where angels delightfully

encourage unforgettable pictures.

My crystal knowledge bridges
provide mind pathways that
separate self from earthly bonds;
I intoxicate mind and soul while
walking through gleaming vineyards,
supernaturally teasing

without waking myself.

Bedtime seeds planted in
dark rooted night toil
escape passive mind howls and
evolve like grain beating machines,
like solutions harvesting answers
as might a would-be Picasso

discover a spiritual pallet realm.

Like Two Lovers

Past seeing minds
mask imagination
kiss waiting and
recognition praying
like an unknown lover
shadow standing.
Dark mind caverns haunt
through dense red and
sunless black.
No sighted end beyond
oceans and mountains exist.
Only unasked questions
guide future answers
dark languishing in
blind minds.
Sweet imagination, a
membrane thickness away,
patiently lingers
like silver and glass,
light and reflection,
thought and discovery,
universe and universe.
It bashfully listens while
humanity sleeps,
kiss waiting and
recognition praying.

Like two lovers,
humanity and imagination,
silhouetted on cavern's
lighted edge,
hold each other as dusk
silently approaches and
withdrawal forever threatens.

Past Dawn and Dusk

Short-sighted Robert has
twenty-four hour reality.
He's an applied continuum with
no relevance past each moment.
He can't measure, reason or
argue past another sunrise.
A fleeting moment might as
well be a fleeting year.
A transitory hour might as
well be a transitory life time.
He can't reflect time's length.
His essence existence
wallows in quicksand time
while a measuring sun
gauges his life's awareness.
He's a short lived phenomenon
in a long living universe.
Sun up to sun down,
spring to summer is
his reality recognition.
His life begins and ends
between awareness and ignorance,
between minutes and hours.
For him there is no measure
except pretending to
understand time and be
foolish enough to think
he can measure it.
His quicksand time too soon
turns into mental mush.

He can only measure
between dawn and dusk.
His illusive life boils down to a
few thoughts, memories and emotions.
He will never grasp time's length
with a mushy mind and a
quicksand time imagination.

Resurrection

Time assaults what was and provokes
quiet minds to dream of what might be.
Modern gardens dwindle.
Few walk faulty planned paths.
Brooding minds fear transformation.
Sweet odors are gone.
Greedy stench pervades.
Weeds dominate gardens.
They've come far to find nothing.
A dichotomy exists between them.
Some are unable to lift a bloom.
Others are unwilling to recreate.
Most have little strength.
They have little patience.
On and on gardens fail to live.
There is no middle ground.
Mending thoughts can't till soil.
Liberty thieves free load.
Sweet melodic spirits play music while
painting time canvases with waiting colors.
Planned paths quietly reappear.
Most were separated and lost.
Weeds decorate sweet nostalgia.
Yesterday has no instinct.
Deep rooted memories emerge.
Hand vicinity strokes new talent.
Sunlight is quietly recognized.
A different morning arises.
Future gardens seek intervention.
Spring breezes soft float caress.
Nature feels her way through.

Anxious sprouting won't wait.
Tolerance seeks gratification.
Born again takes on new meaning.
Garden societies validate nature.
Everyone accepts resurrection.

So Much to Learn

Time is a
spiteful measuring tool that
must be organized.
It's a
means for growing life
with innovative minds.
It's a
self disciplinary tool for
keeping promises.
It's a
learning tool for
keeping track of events.
It's a
way and means for
life management.
It's a
human invention that
circumvents internal clocks.
It's a
profound thing that
punishes human idleness.
It's a
much to learn about thing that
harasses everything.

Time Erodes

Rain soaked decaying debris odor just outside a cabin door
invokes thought as lifeless limbs and logs downstream
river float.

Spring reminding flowers flourish and green grass gets greener
with each passing day as time speaks its mind like a
newborn murmurs.

Inspired Cottonwood trees humbly bend towards rushing
river with half exposed roots, they grasp like edifices
wishing hopeful endurance.

They bravely clutch muddy banks as rain kisses, but
accumulates into angry streams and rivers acting like giant
rough watery hands.

Everything bends, bows and seeks false security like a man
trying to remain alive by futilely grasping and squeezing
life to death.

Eyes fill with nature seeking herself as a mindless river erodes
banks, uncovering history and unveiling earth's soul with
careless ease.

Eaten away present day banks silently complain as rushing
water exposes old clam shells, broken glass pieces and
human historical artifacts.

Buried humanity is slightly revealed in a silted river bank melting away a known past before awakened eyes.

Nature discovers, erodes and resurrects forgotten life history one storm at a time like a man unveils inner self one furtive word at a time.

Moment's Stretch

Time is a moment long.
It practices nothing,
remains an enigma.
Extended moments
stretch into seasons
like leaves passing,
snow melting and
life decaying into

organic material,
souls meandering towards

waiting faces.

Time is ignorant.
It processes nothing,
only pretend counts
moments into lives.
It counts how many
have been known,
loved, fallen and
how many have

been buried,
processed and absorbed into a

moment's stretch.

Time Has No Conscience

I

Plants grew in
my attended garden.
Things were easy while
I ate breakfast and
leisurely said good-by to
morning light.
Too soon there was
nothing to eat and
nowhere to sit.
Unwilling flowers
bloomed
too early in spring.
Fruit perished on
wilted vines.
I blamed
Mother Nature for
tricking and fooling
me into thinking
time was surely
benevolent and
on my side.

II

Timely thoughts are
simple guidelines,
but useless
freedom tilling tools.
They waft in
fantasy flight
like near weightless
pollen drifting
beyond and through,
over and under
until random ignorance
collects them.
And like a forgotten
note found or an
unnoticed life changed,
timely thoughts have
no content and are
immediately obsolete.
Deep down where
dragons live and
dreams are born,
where wars end and
friendships begin,
patient liberty tools are
judiciously placed in
appropriate timely hands.

III

Life with earth is an
uncertain thing.
It waits like
imaginary time,
waits like a
lost relative at a
half opened front door.
It wishes to be
invited in with
kindness and grace.
It wishes to be fed,
put to bed and
kissed good night.
Time has no tactics,
arguments or suggestions.
Its purpose is to pass
while aging everything.
It likes to make
strong men weep and
weak men pray for
one more moment.
Time has no plans,
dreams or desires.
It passes with no regrets,
apologies or sadness.

A Million Thoughts Beneath

A mind can
misplace long ago
unpleasant experiences in
corners and creases, in
veiled black painted gathering rooms.
A million absent
thoughts are securely
buried beneath a
mountain of living.
A melancholy lifetime seeps
disorder and confusion.
Morning seeks arcing day sun.
Enlightenment carries
sane liability towards
mystic evening and recreated night.
Years ago is a split second revelation.
Time between day and night
lasts a moment.
Day breaks in disordered
black collecting rooms,
brain creases and
thus in a continuum mind.
Exposed memories are like a
thousand tiny hammers
breaking down tall wide
constructed stone barriers.

A lifetime world can
unwillingly crumble beneath
unpleasant experiences
subconsciously well placed,
instinctively mortared together,
methodically psyche protected.
And yet with destroyed
stone barrier remnants,
revelation bridges are built and
over without hesitation
new tomorrows are traveled.

Life

Life exposes as wisdom lines reflect.

Another's Hand

Pure white snow silently
falls on roadway black as
tires tenuously grip,
insecurity evolves quickly.

Two people listen only to an
auto engine quietly hum,
feeling heater warmth, with no
appreciative words spoken.

In near suspicious distance
two thousand pounds of
automobile monster heads with
white skin and black feet.

Eyes and mind dart for
three frantic seconds and
perceived disaster strikes as
options quickly fade.

White and beige metal embrace,
airbags boom as once wide eyes in
blackness fails to see, then
silence and burnt hydrogen odor.

Immeasurable moments
pass agonizingly slow as a
driver painfully makes way
out and around to his wife.

How ironic timing
sees her way in and out of
trouble momentarily, yet
plans schemes far in advance.

Courage

High cliff leaping fear
evokes common sense.
Courage evades
ledge standing feet.
Raging quandaries
quietly perceive time.
Souls deciding freedom
fill homecoming spirits.
Tear filled dawn eyes
alter moving views.

And yet high cliffs wait as if
time might stand still.
Undefined cowardly ways
make men tremble.
Defined bravery
makes men weep.
Tomorrow walks with
eyes open, feet moving and
seemingly with
decisions already concluded.

Courage passes through
fearful watery blue,
below common sense and
through spaced membranes.
It reflects decisions like
silver backed glass.
Echoing mirrored minds
reveal authentic truth.
Genuine courage leaps
fear cliffs with timely resolution.

Down Country Club Road

I now alone linger sit
on a swing for two,
pushing back and forth,
half aware and worthlessly
thinking about when I ran.
My open arms wishfully
reach out to touch and
hold someone running towards.
My hands are like
frosty warm breath
seen on a cold afternoon.
I allow arms to mentally inhale,
accept tolerant grace and
refresh my aging spirit.
I exhale inevitable change.
Shadowy trees pass to left and
emerging spring daffodils
pass quickly to right.
Nature's peculiar breath
feeds my waning optimism.
I'm like a captured philosophy
with no place to course
except onward down
Country Club Road at
least one more time.
I wish to speak
my enigmatic mind,
express feelings and
exchange passion.

I wish to write about it
with poetic grace, to
bring it forth from mind to
reality as I balance in a
Zen state of mind.
My swing is still.
My mind is at ease.
I only mind run nowadays.

Face Signatures

I see broken sticks
Bent at dead angles
With no purpose for
Better days are gone.
And while bark peals and
Deep parts get exposed,
Turning twilight gray
On a cold flat slab
Is life converting.
I see dirty gray
Snow quantity deep
With no purpose as
Better days are gone.
Slow brown melting snow
Rightly heavy from
Lack of fresh air
Fears being altered
Into living water.
I see my gaunt face
Aging too fast as
Emerging signature lines
Echo better days gap.
Life exposes and
Wisdom lines reflect.
I see in dim eyes a
Glow yet remains as
Time evolves itself.
I see other hands
Reaching and grasping,
Willing to help and
Much stronger than mine.

Young minds indeed seek
Broken angled sticks,
Fast melting snow and
Past face signatures that
In truth transforms life.

Falling Life

Through air a rose petal gracefully floats towards earth, leaving
all hope behind, surrendering to forces beyond control.

Downward it floats with mindless reality, not knowing its
fate, not knowing its destination as a life essence piece.

Rose bushes say good-by to self parts, from bud to rose,
from petal to death, life makes known again and again its
intentions.

o

A man is different, blessed with mind and soul; he floats with
known questions and a bit of understanding.

Through air he drifts with dying disconnect, with unknown
assurance, with drifting departure speculation felt.

He hears a drifting song whether wind whispered or spiritually
sang and finally senses a reassuring melody.

o

Sing on sweet unknown angels who weigh wind and gravity,
and find transitional places for rose petals and men.

Sing on spirits who gently grasp and hold all things dear, and
tenderly rest life essence with conceived compassion.

Heed that drifting melodic sweet substance that to earth drifts,
for in a man's falling there comes rising creation knowledge.

History Book Pages

It's like an
unheard whisper, an
unscratched itch, a
weird thought that haunts.
It's like an
unanswered question, an
unread book, an
unseen art work that
conjures desired self images.
It isn't like an
understood direction, a
recognized path, a
well drawn map from which
our lives are lived.
We speak minds,
write books and
paint our canvases.
We learn to crawl,
walk and run in
own directions with
own maps and
own pumping blood.
We sooner or later
realize that we're
only a whisper, an
itch, a haunting self image
being created as if
in another's mind.

We fill own blank
history book pages with
words and pictures, with
ideas and dreams, with
plans and maps that
few if any will ever see or
life appreciate.
And yet we do this as if
someone really cares.

Life's Worst

I've truly walked a
shadowy death valley and
felt life's worst.
And when hurt,
frustration and
trouble now come,
I fear not
outcomes for
I've ground
my knuckles in
life's black
contributing face.
I've ridden a train to
hell and back.
I've sailed a ship to
death island.
Tell me not
how badly you feel for
I know how badly
you could feel.
I'm not alone
knowing
high plane standing in
deep despair, however,
few know physical and
mental pain
beyond imagination.
Loss of a child
sears mind and soul,
tears heart and spirit,
bleeds truth into reality.

Life is understandable
no matter what
happens when one
knows worst for
best yet to come is
expected.

Oh, Sweet Blue Bird

I made a
blue bird dance,
sought moon light,
heard a willow weep.
And when that was all done,
I built a dam,
made a motorcycle roar,
kissed my lover's lips.
And when that was all done,
I awoke to know
it was only a dream and
I had no lover, bike or
desire to work.
When and where did
I leave myself?
Out there on a road to
nowhere I guess.
I fell behind
day after day,
year after year until
I couldn't see a
path to follow.
Now here I am
left with only dreams.
Oh, sweet blue bird
bury me under a
willow tree in
moon light and
let me start again
until I get it right.

Pain Wouldn't Diminish

I walked onward towards
goals in concrete set,
in stone carved and
in mind long dreamed.
My lower back wouldn't
excuse itself from pain.
Pain sought its own end
without explanation or excuse.
I walked, lifted and bent
without bowing to
its relentless pursuit.

It couldn't diminish
my dreams.
I worked through pain until
completion patted my back,
soothed my soul,
gave me a passing grade.
Life for me was an
educational thing, but
I didn't know it would
painfully educate me for
ten-thousand years.

I was back stab murdered
last time here.
A small skin blemish
itches occasionally and
reminds me of that
previous life's ending.

I've learned that there's
no end to pain.
God is an awesome
teacher and rings a
mean school bell.

I life digressed through
soul and spirit,
seeking what was until
I found myself in a womb
one first time.
From whispers
I discovered life.
I established essence
through waving energy.
In one gleaming moment
I became alive.

I ultimately found
no concrete set or
carved in stone goals, only
flowing dreams established by
energetic whispers.
One constant became clear,
pain could not be avoided.
It was just a matter of
where and when
it would inflict an
insistent will to be.

My back pain was a
time awareness provoker.
It was a humility
causing burden.

I ultimately found myself
bowing to its relentless pursuit.
It taught humility and grace, and
finally gave me living joy.
I accepted my own
explanations and excuses through
pain's insistent reincarnation.

Passing Moments

So many times
silent minutes
pass without notice for
knowing you're here is enough.
Yet when you're away
they pass noticeably slow.
I sit now in quiet space
passing dragging moments,
introspectively listening and
noticing sunlight lecture.
It teaches history,
mathematics and astronomy.
I hear it weep and bow to
forces beyond its control.
I hear it for you have
taught me how to listen.
I hear it for you have
been lovingly silent.
It now disappears beyond
sun porch windows where
we gazed at our
whispering river flow
with wordless expression.
And now I wish to speak to
say I miss you and
you are not here.
Join me soon to
listen and observe at
river's constant edge.
Let us watch time pass
beyond today's glow.

Speak to me with
your eyes when next
we grasp fast moving
time quietly together.

Political Confidence

I gain confusion from
podium speakers
towering above me,
lecturing and imparting
knowledge with confidence, and
yet, I fear they are ignorant of
true life meaning and
standards set by those
who before commanded respect.
Confidence is a buttery spread
laid on thick and gets
slicker and slicker as
audiences gather larger and
personalities suppress facts.

I gain understanding
more from within as
experience, history and
facts seep from my world.
And then there's that
little voice that whispers with
no agenda as a
good teacher should.
I fear our status is
becoming too statistical.
I fear confidence is
becoming too confidential.
I fear politics is
becoming too political.

Rock and Roll is Here to Stay

Good night sweet lullaby.
I can't listen to you tonight.
You disguise yourself in
many ways,
pretending to be
my friend and
impart adoration.
My dreams will
swell like angry seas,
my mind will
face trumpets seeking
my end and
I fear morning will arrive
without realized fanfare.

I drift so easily in
my overstuffed chair,
half watching television, but
when I slid into bed;
my mind begins to
engage thoughts,
ideas and schemes.
Good night sweet lullaby.
You're a short lived grace
I seldom embrace for
sleep comes hard and
rest is nearly impossible.
Dreams are my
only conciliation.

I live an active life
day and night.
My realized time is
nearly twice a long for
I am moment aware
day and night.
So when music
threatens to end and
movies begin,
I whisper
good night sweet lullaby.
Rock and roll is
here to stay.

So in my quest for sleep,
dreaming interferes and
night becomes alive.
For in my disorder
comes order.
I sleep-dream-sleep,
sleep-dream sleep, then
write in awakened morning.
I embellish and rewrite
night's remembered fantasy.
I reluctantly say good-by to
sweet lullaby, but then
"rock and roll" is
in my blood.

The Sound of Death

A bugle blares in
misty mind reeking
fear born from
somewhere deep
within and past reality,
down into illusion,
down from a
dug deep black hole.
It hurts realism,
bends humanity and
weakens sanity.

Who blows that
shiny bugle,
presses those lips
against and spits air
through a restricting
little opening that
squeezes nothing into
something?

That bugle music
played by an unknown
mystic being is a
farewell to life and a
haunting hello to death.
Too many hear
forlorn taps played.
Too many experience
bitter reality,
bent humanity and
weakened sanity.

Quiet Child

Child be quiet.
 Sunlight smiles in your eyes.
  Clever thoughts will meet you
   When clocks watch and
    Calendar months don't get torn.
     Oh sweet child hear music
      Where Mother sits and
       Father doesn't go.
        I found pictures of
         Yesterday's blues that
          Had much to love.

Your sister is glory gone.
 Brother lives too far away.
  Family matters, but
   I feel sad for you anyway.
    I can't help you grow because
     I'm in between now and then.
      Can you feel my tears
       When I walk another way
        Past your chosen silence?
         I can find a better way to dance, but
          Don't know another mind.

Oh sweet flower bloom with
  Bright and right eyes.
  I promise to teach
  If chance gives and
  I learn to not weep badly.
  So be quiet and
  Listen to tardy time.
  You are sunlight that
  Slowly grows nearer.
  I want loving and
  Want it today.

Sweet Life

Echoes and sunlight
crowd my mind.
I can't see
tomorrow for today.
I'm blind with
ideas and
deaf to suggestions.
Fascination beats an
empty candy sack that
won't fill.
Blindness and
deafness are
attributes for a man
who sometimes
thinks too much.
Big plans wait on a
drawing board
next to a computer
placed on a desk
full of money.
I'm blind with
ideas and
deaf to suggestions.
Somehow, someway,
somewhere, sometime,
I futilely lost
my sense of taste.
Life isn't sweet
anymore.

Was Better Available

We melancholy think
we could have done better and
feel humbly discontented.
However, many cannot
think, but proudly feel.

Oh arrogant confidence
you are a sly one with
your false impressions and
distorted mirror images.
And late at night
when others are in bed,
haughty confidence
you soothe souls and
pretend you can love.
A disfigured world brings
false beauty to surface.

So it seems in that
oval office, men
whisper and pretend they are
greater than they truly are.
Maybe it's necessary.
Maybe history chooses
great ones for that
early morning mirror and that
late night shadowed room.
Sometimes this is so, but
sometimes humanity is truth blind.

Therein lies our mirrored
melancholy thinking.
Maybe we could have
done better or maybe
better was not available.

Welder Roger Beck

Roger Beck sometimes used protective welding equipment,
but most times expediency beat odds with precarious skill.

He used broken helmet glass held with pliers at a strategic
distance while welding arcs.

His smoke colored eyes moved and saw everything as if life
was forever and he was in charge.

He welded steel frames for fabricated colored woven wire
planes that shimmered as perpetual organic clocks.

He believed AC and DC electricity could surge through these
pyramid shapes to record time in any Milky Way space.

He had no conception of time, yet built a universal clock and
had no appreciation for beauty, yet built a brilliant piece of art.

He valued life, yet smoked cigarettes with a nicotine addiction
as if having no knowledge of black lung disease or cancer.

He ignored art and beauty while striking arcs and melting
three metals together to form a perfect single union.

He spent time joining thick and thin steel with precise hot
carbon arcs as bright as a noon day sun.

Roger Beck lived in a dim dirty shop full of sketches, strategies,
sculptures and unfinished metal projects.

Some day he might convert to MIG and TIG and other exotic
forms of welding, but for now a simple stick welder was he.

Risk

Risk lies on a pillow
beside everyone's head,
never sleeps or
seeks relief.
It gives and takes with
reservation and intrigue.
Illusive risk management
most times defies reason.
Things to worry or
not worry about are
usually upside down,
put on a list wrong,
confused with real peril.
Fear and anxiety,
stretch imagination beyond
where it should be and
causes stress and despair or
confidence and exhilaration.
Risk wills out
whether good or bad,
imagined or real.
It always finds a home
in an anxious mind and
lies on a pillow
beside everyone's head.

Celebration

I either know a
lot about
what doesn't matter or a
little bit about
what does matter.
To know what needs
knowing is heaven
waiting for such as me.

Leave me alone in
my ignorance I plead.
I have learned this
from a higher source,
don't ask me how,
except life has
taught me and
I have learned to listen.

Gathered simplicity
spiritually teaches well.
An important rain drop
cannot be found in an
immense ocean,
yet frequently unearthed
when one is thirst dying
on an insistent desert.

I am either a dry desert or a
water drop waiting detection.
Of this ignorance
I cannot be dissuaded for
spiritual knowledge
comes awkwardly hard.
Of this I can only celebrate
its faithful uncertainty.

Small Town Hero

A small town hero
lives nearby.
A one arm,
eighty four year old man
peddles around town on
worn out chains and
worn out tires.
His wear shows
like that tricycle.
He continues rounds
persistently collecting empty
aluminum cans for recycling.
He mowed my lawn with
one arm yesterday.
He got all cleaned and
dressed up for a funeral today,
not his own, someone younger.
His spirit shines
beneath rough exterior, in
wispy speech and
short story telling.
Youth lost at WPA camp,
arm lost in an explosion,
wife lost to cancer,
skin and bone lost to hard work.
Now in later years
music yet plays in his soul as
one hand guides body while
brown eyes see rare direction.

Uniqueness causes smiles,
strength gives faith,
old age bestows hope.
All this bound in a
one old man
seeking nothing but life
hour by hour, day by day.

I'll Get You

Days pass, nights fall,
seasons sneak past attention.
I can't hear life grinding as
it silently leaves
my bones, skin and inner parts.

Dusty picture albums whisper,
reminding and annoying,
causing melancholy thoughts.
Their bound resting pictures
foster vivid mind movies.

Reality discloses a
quiet message.
I can hear, smell and taste it,
knowing that it requests
my undivided attention.

Old jazz record albums on
edge stand near with
moldy odor and worn corners.
They also whisper, wishing to
play and sing again.

Used depressed textbooks
stacked upon each other lay
neglected and sorrowful,
knowing that possessed knowledge is
mostly out of date and useless.

I recall life with few assets and
how I collected things over
numerous energetic years.
And now with new playthings
I reside with a different mind.

I'm now taking new pictures,
buying new music,
reading new books and yet
I'm not a new man, but an
old man with new interests.

I yet cannot hear life grinding, but
suspect it's out there and
in here whispering,
"I'll get you and
sooner or later you're mine."